The Golden Stag

David Spencer

Copyright © 2021 by David Spencer & Marilyn Spencer

ISBN: 978-1-951670-22-1 (paperback)
ISBN: 978-1-951670-23-8 (ePub)

All rights reserved. No part of this publication may be reproduced, distributed, or transmitted in any form or by any electronic or mechanical means, without the prior written permission of the publisher, except in the case of brief quotations embodied in critical reviews and certain other noncommercial uses permitted by copyright law.

Ordering Information:
For orders and inquiries, please contact: books@authorsnote360.com
www.authorsnote360.com

Printed in the United States of America

Contents

Dedication vii
ACKNOWLEDGEMENT viii
FOREWORD 2
EPILOGUE 13
POST-SCRIPT 15

Dedication

Henry Harry Szpejnowski

June 17, 1923

February 14, 1973

Dedicated to the Memory of my Father,
Henry H. Szpejnowski, 1923–1973

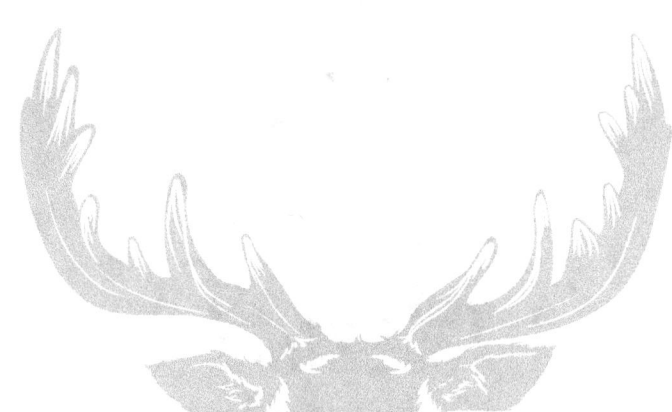

ACKNOWLEDGEMENT

Writing a book is a journey. It needs imagination, motivation and of course passion. Publishing my books will not be realized without the support of the people around me.

I'd like to start with Emma Reading (My Wife's Mother) for all the compliments and words of encouragement she has given me. Her words served as my guide to the right direction in writing.

To my very good friends Sam Wilson and Jeff Yelton for all the support they have shown and for pushing me to work on my book.

To our family friends:
- Sandy and Fred Hardy
- Tim and Carol Dionne

Our family is so blessed to have a family friend like you. Always remember that you are always dear to our family.

To my Publisher Author's Note 360, I thank you for showing interest and for believing in my book. I thank the whole team for making this republication possible.

Finally, I dedicate this book to my beautiful and ever supportive wife Marilyn Spencer, the LOVE OF MY LIFE. She's been a huge fan of my books and she supported me all the way. She stood by me in sickness and in health. She's always been the source of my strength and my inspiration. Without her, I'm not sure if I'd be able to finish even a single book. To my beloved Marilyn, I thank you and I love you so much.

FOREWORD

IN 1947, A team of Russian archeologists excavated an ancient tomb in what had been a northern province of the Assyrian Empire. That same year, the Dead Sea Scrolls had been found in the Qumran Caves of Israel. The Russian site was at Ziwiyeh, in the territory of a mountain people the Assyrians had called the Mannai. They were known to historians as the Mannaeans.

The archeologists had come to this spot after working at several sites in Soviet Armenia. In the time of the Assyrians, Armenia was called "Urartu". The team had found extensive evidence of nomadic Scythian attacks and devastation at the Armenian digs. Now, they were working near the border of Azerbaijan and Kurdistan, west of Lake Urmia.

Stefan Sulimirsky of the University of Moscow supervised the digging. Henryk Szpejnowski from the University of Krakow in Poland carefully brushed off the objects that would be sent to the Hermitage Museum. Along with the golden artifacts left behind by a race of nomad warriors from the distant past, the scientists discovered a leather scroll in a bronze box.

Written on the scroll were words in an ancient Indo-European language known to the archaeologists. It was the story of a people long supposed to have no record of their own. It was the story of their existence on the Russian steppes, and in the Crimea. Combined with information from the Assyrian archives, it provided a clearer picture of their role in history.

The Polish scientist made his first note: "This story began 674 years before the birth of Christ..." The text read:

The sound was barely audible, like the gentle noise made by the metal horse-trappings, as the muscles of the animals lurched slowly forward with the movement of their hooves. In late autumn, the tall feather-grass of the steppes was dried out, giving way to the hooves unwillingly.

The Nomad cavalry came upon a huge burial kurgan, worn away by time. The top layer of the earthen mound had been blown away by the wind of the steppes, exposing the Royal death-guard of a fallen king. The riders who were still erect sat upon the saddled bones of their horses. Tattered remnants of clothing that still clung to the bodies of the death-guard fluttered in the wind. Small silver bells hung from their horses, from the worn leather death-masks of their mounts. As the bells moved with the wind, they played a hollow, haunting tune.

Dawn on the northern shore of the Black Sea, on the Kuban River Delta. Tent-nomads take their herds to pasture, as horse-bowmen ride the steppes. At the Royal encampment of the Nomads, the god of the sun gleamed from the golden stag on the shield of their king. The floor of the Nomad Kings' tent was covered with a colorful carpet, decorated with lions and stags. Enemy skulls that had been hollowed out, filled with molten gold and bound with leather were lined up against the wall of the Royal tent as drinking cups. Scalps hung from the bridles of the Nomad Chieftans.

In our nomad language, my name means, "The Sacred Ways". It is said that the Nomad people of the steppes have no written language. Therefore, we have no story. I, a Shaman of the Nomad people will put down the story of the wedding - alliance with the King of the Valley People, the ruler of the Royal City. I will put the story down, upon this scroll.

To the sun-baked, mountainous south was Assyria ... land of the valley of the rivers, of the gates of Nineveh with its Winged Bulls. These were the words of the King of the Valley People, the ruler of the Royal City, in a prayer to Shamash, his Sun-god:

"Regarding Partatua, King of the Iskuza who has just sent his ambassador to Esarhaddon, King of Assyria, about a princess I ask you Shamash, great lord, if Esarhaddon gives a princess to Partatua King of the Iskuza for a wife, whether Partatua will observe and keep his oath to Esarhaddon, King of Assyria?"

The wind on the steppes blew gently across the tall grass, making the plains look like an endless field of flowing wheat in the bright autumn sun. Papoeus waited in the feather - grass with his bow drawn, an arrow fitted at the ready. His Mongol pony, the color of the earth, was on its knees. Scalps hung from its bridle. Above the top of waving grass, he could see the crest of the Black Robes' conical metal helmet gleaming in the sun. He saw the shoulders of the enemy tribesman Ukko cloaked in black, moving with the motion of his horse.

The Black Robe Chieftan Ukko rode along slowly with his Warrior-Prince Ahti, at the head of a raiding party. Their Warrior-Shaman Tapio, named for their god of the forests rode at the rear of their band.

When his enemy was in range, Papoeus let loose his arrow. The missile struck Ukko in the chest with force, and with finality. With the death of the Black Robe Chieftan, the rest of the Nomad Saka bowmen sprang from the grass, firing their bows as they charged. Ahti and Tapio had their swords drawn, and moved to meet them head on. The Nomads, having fired their first arrows, stopped suddenly as if to ride away. They turned their mounts to fire over their shoulders, striking many more Black Robes.

Again the Saka Bowmen turned their mounts around and charged forward, firing yet more arrows. They repeated this "mock-retreat" tactic until they had worn Ahti's forces down. The Warrior-Prince and his Shaman had one choice, and that was to retreat. Papoeus rode back to where Ukko lay on the steppes. He slid casually down from his saddle, and with a few quick motions of his knife took the scalp. The horse-bowman Papoeus was named for the father of the gods. He rode into his home-camp, on the shore of the Kuban River. His wife Apia had been named for the goddess of the earth. She was at their camp-fire preparing their mid-day meal, pouring some mares' milk into a cup for their young son, Leipoxais.

The son of Papoeus was playing next to their house-wagon. The warrior dismounted, leaving his pony near their tent. He bent down to pick up Leipoxais, lifting him high into the air shouting, "Upada ...up you go!"

As great as the Empire of the Valley King Esarhaddon was, he needed our help against his enemies, and also against our ancient enemies of the steppes, the outcast Gimmirai. A daughter of the house of the Valley King was named after a goddess. Her brother the Prince was called, "Ashur- Creates-a-Son." Because his sister, the Princess, "Goddess-Sherua is-the-one-who-saves" was the grand-daughter of the Queen Mother, she was truly of the Royal line.

These were the words of the Assyrian Princess in a letter to the wife of her brother, Ashur-Creates-a-Son:

"... while you are only a daughter-in-law, the lady of the house of Ashur-Banipal, the eldest son of the King born in the official residence of Esarhaddon, King of Assyria ... after all, I, Sherua - Eterat, am the eldest daughter born in the official residence to Esarhaddon, the great and legitimate King, King of the world, King of Assyria."

Our Nomad King's envoy to the Court of the Valley King was Arpoxais, one of our Chieftans from the steppes, from the Royal House of the Crimea. We had come riding down through the mountain passes, down between the two great inland oceans. We rode ever southward, all the way past Lake Urmia in Armenia to the Valley of the Tigris River, and up to the gates of the Royal City of the King of the Valley People.

At those gates of Nineveh, I stood as though transfixed; spellbound, looking up ever higher to the great stone statues of the sacred Winged Bulls, the Lamassi. The god of the sun of our Nomad Sakas is carried through the heavens on the horns of the Golden Stag; we had nothing like this, to show the deity of our kings. The winged Lamassu had long, muscular legs with the hooves of bulls or the paws of lions, making the statues look like powerful animals in their stride.

The great stone wings made the gods look as though they were in flight, like some kind of giant eagles. High above the wings, the rock-hard gods wore the tall Royal Assyrian crowns, as did King Esarhaddon and Prince Ashur-Banipal. The winged gods had the faces of the kings of Ashur, and the long, stony beards combined the strength of the bulls and the lions with the deity of the Royal House of Assyria.

Our cavalry camped outside of the gates of Nineveh. Our tents and our camp-fires stretched out as far as the people of the city could see. The horses rested in our huge camp in their thousands. I walked through part of the herd, choosing one of our Royal stallions as a sacrifice. I had to ensure that the gods would approve of our alliance with the Assyrians. I led the horse to a spot where one of the Winged Bulls stood guard at the gate.

While some of the men secured the stallion with long ropes, I took another length of hemp and a wooden stick. With the middle of my rope wrapped and knotted around the wood, the ends of it were tied around the animal's neck. I grasped the stick firmly in my hands, and began twisting and tightening the strand fastened to the sacrifice. The stallion naturally bolted to get free, but the men with their ropes held it fast.

All the while, I was turning the rope with all of my might. All the while, I was praying to the father of the gods, and the god of the sun. I twisted and twisted the stick, slowly making the rope tighter with each turn. The hemp was so strong, and it applied so much pressure to the throat of the horse that it eventually went down in heap ... eyes wide, legs thrashing.

(At this point, Stefan Sulimirsky took a break from analyzing the text of the scroll. It was painstaking work, using a magnifying glass to make out some of the characters. Stefan himself was an Assyriologist, and an expert in ancient Central Asian languages. Henryk had specialized in Eastern European dialects at the University of Krakow. When neither of them could decipher a word or a passage, they referred to an old German textbook from the 1890's.

While Henryk took over examining the scroll, his Russian partner Stefan catalogued a find from the day's dig. It was a golden stag, unbroken and beautiful. He thought that possibly it had been made by one of the Greek colonists of the Black Sea area, about 500 B.C. If so, it had come either from Olbia or Sinope. This site was important to Stefan, because he had long considered himself to be a descendant of the nomadic Scythians. That is why he became interested in archaeology in the first place. It seemed to him now that he was looking straight into the face of his ancestry.

He wrote, "The article is an ornament, used in the Scythian religion. The hind quarters of this golden animal are raised slightly, with the back legs pointing forward. The front legs are folded under the muscular metal body of the stag and pointed backwards, giving the illusion of movement. The front and back hooves meet under the sculpture, welded together.

The stylized curling row representing the antlers of the stag run all the way from the rear of its body to the top of its head. The neck is elongated, and the head is lifted up, adding to the illusion of motion or flight." After making his notes, Sulimirsky went back to the scroll)...

The Assyrian King was given a rich store of Bulgar furs to seal the bargain. The ceremony to seal the wedding-alliance between the daughter of Esarhaddon and our King Bartatua took place within the walls of the Royal City, near the Tigris River, in the shadow of the mountains. The Assyrian King and the Queen Mother Nagiya-Zakutu sat with the Assyrian Princess. Prince Ashur-Banipal sat with his wife, the Lady Ashur-Sharrat.

The wife of Ashur-Banipal spent much of the ceremony quietly gloating over the fate of the Assyrian Princess. Her rival from the Royal Court would have to travel in an ox-cart, living in a tent in a primitive northern land many miles away. As the wife of the future King of Assyria, the Lady Ashur-Sharrat would live in the palaces of Nineveh. The daughter of Esarhaddon would be married to a Nomad King who was nothing more than a bearded mercenary, a savage war-lord hired by her father-in-law.

The Princess would probably insist on remaining in Nineveh. Bartatua, though, would never allow that as a condition of the alliance. The only compromise in taking his bride north to the steppes would be to have her live in our base-camp of Sakkiz, in Armenia. The Lady Ashur-Sharrat hoped that she would never see the Assyrian Princess again.

Arad Nana, the servant of Esarhaddon was in attendance; Ashur-Shallim, another servant of his king was at Court. Adad-shumi-usur and Ibashshi-ilu, other members of the Royal House, stood in the rear of the room behind the Valley Kings' priests. As Shaman of the Royal Saka tribe of the Scoloti, I accompanied King Bartatua, as did our Royal envoy Arpoxais. The High Priest of Esarhaddon, servant of their supreme god Ashur and their sun-god Shamash came forward, saying,

"Shamash, great lord, you rule from your throne and see everything on earth. At dawn, the eastern portals open, and you are seen in the sky. Through your children Kittu and Misharu, justice is done and the laws are kept. I ask you, Shamash, great lord, to give many, many blessings to King Partatua of the Iskuza, and the daughter of his majesty King Esarhaddon! May this alliance protect our King and this city of Nineveh from our enemies the Madai!"

Prayers were given up to the Assyrian gods Nabu and Marduk; to their deities Sin, Bel, and Ishtar of Nineveh; to the god Ninurta and the goddess Gula; to the god Nergal, and the goddess Ningal. More prayers were said to Shamash, and to Ashur, their king of the gods. I myself offered prayers to the father of our gods, Papoeus; to our god of the sun, Oetosyrus and to our goddess of the earth, Apia.

As our Saka cavalry left the city of Nineveh, the people watched as we rode by in our numbers, with our high pointed riding caps over our beards. Our legs, which hung from the sides of our horses, were covered by our long trousers. The large leather cases that held our bows and arrows were at the sides of our saddles as we rode.

As the people saw our Nomad cavalry thundering by, they must have been glad to see us leave their city. Armed with our bows and arrows, and with our Median style short-swords, we must have posed a danger of destruction to them, able to strike at any time. And we were just that.

On our way back north, we stopped in the mountains of the Mannai, to the west of Lake Urmia. We made our camp at the top of a hill, in the village of Ziwiyeh. This place was one day's ride east of our base-camp in Sakkiz. At Ziwiyeh I, the Scoloti Shaman Exampaeus, called, "the Sacred Ways" knelt by a fire. Giving up prayers to Papoeus, the father of the gods and to the mother - goddess Tabiti, I turned my knife over and over in my leathery fingers.

I held the blade of the knife up to the sky so as to see the sun, Oetosyrus, shining brightly behind it. I stood beside Bartatua's Royal Shield of the Golden Stag and said, "Oetosyrus, the Sacred Stag is your symbol. You are carried across the sky by his horns. I leave this scroll, the story of the alliance between Esarhaddon of Assyria and our King Bartatua in this place in your honor."

The Assyrian Princess was now our Saka Queen. Mile after endless mile, Bartatua's wife rode in the Royal wagon, up from the Tigris River Valley. She traveled past Lake Urmia and Sakkiz, up through the pass of the Caucasus Mountains, riding through the lands between the two great inland oceans, the Black Sea and the Caspian Sea. The Saka Queen rode all the way to her new home in the Crimea, all the way to the steppes, the vast prairies of our homeland. The one who had been the Princess of Nineveh sat in the Royal wagon of Bartatua, looking back to the south as long as she could, until both the sight and the memory of her past was gone from her forever.

For a second time, the Black Robe Prince Ahti and the Shaman Tapio crossed over into our territory on the Kuban River Delta. From his base in the Crimea, King Bartatua directed that these raiders be driven from the steppes. Having seen our "mock retreat" tactic before, Ahti decided to avoid contact with our horse-bowmen. He had it in mind to raid one of our farmer-tribes, and return to his homeland in the west.

The Black Robes were crossing the wetlands of the delta, when they were confronted by our mobile Nomad cavalry. He had made the mistake of underestimating the amount of ground that we could cover in a short period of time. Ahti must have known then that his position was hopeless. Rather than flee, the Black Robe leader straightened his cloak, adjusted his helmet firmly, and drew his sword.

The resounding clash of forces was inevitable, as was the outcome. Our horsemen charged forward as before, firing their arrows. They pulled up on their reins, turning in their saddles as if to retreat. Once again, arrows were fired over the shoulders of the warriors, and the backs of their mounts with effect. The Sakas were victorious of course. They moved in for the kill, without mercy. I myself rode up to where the enemy bodies lay when our warriors fought no more. In preparation for this moment, I and the other Shamen of the tribe brought several ox-carts.

I found the body of my counter-part Tapio, lying face down with an arrow in his back. Although I could not comprehend his strange belief of worshiping sprits within the trees of the forests, he was still a priest of his people, as I was. I stood beside Tapio with my palms turned upward, my eyes looking to his god of the Sky. I softly said, "Pata... dead."

Ahti had already been scalped, his throat cut. The fallen Black Robes were put into the carts, covered with brush-wood. Chanting his prayers, the ancient Shaman Thamimasadas set the carts on fire, believing that our enemies would serve as a sacrifice to the gods.

Immediately, the startled oxen opened their eyes wide with the sight of the flames crackling behind them. Their nostrils flared with the first hint of the smoke. We let them bolt forward, attached to the wagons securely by their yokes. The teams of oxen lumbered forward frantically, trying to shake off their burning loads to no avail. As they charged aimlessly across the wetlands, they were like so many ghostly fireballs. Eventually, mercifully, the ox-carts were consumed by the raging flames as the animals crashed to their knees on the marshy ground.

Dusk on the northern shore of the Black Sea, on the Kuban River Delta. The sun that gleams from the Royal Shield of the Golden Stag leaves the steppes and the goddess of the moon, Artimpassa comes. The Nomads, a flowing sea of horse-bowmen, of black felt tents and ox-drawn house-wagons, vanish in the frozen sea of time.

THE POLISH ARCHAEOLOGIST Henryk Szpejnowski lit the lantern in his tent. It was the last evening, at end of the dig. He carefully placed the ancient scroll in a wooden crate, and made his final notes. "It is now the year 1947 A.D. Over 2500 years have gone by since the Scythian Shaman left the scroll at here at Ziwiyeh. Twenty one years after the Scytho-Assyrian alliance King Ashur-Banipal, the son of Esarhaddon would enlist the help of the nomad Prince Madyas against the Median King Phraortes and his allies.

That Prince was the son of Bartatua and the Assyrian Princess; he would fight against the "Madai" and the "Gimirrai", handing them a crushing defeat. Twelve years after the death of his Assyrian uncle Ashur-Banipal, Madyas would join with the Medes and Babylonians to destroy the Royal Assyrian City. There was a span of only fifty two years between the time of the wedding - alliance, and the fall of Nineveh." Henryk put down his notepad. He gave a last look at the Scroll of Exampaeus, and the Royal Golden Stag.

*Author's footnote: The Scythians were displaced on the Russian Steppes by their nomadic kinsmen the Sarmatae, about 110 B.C. These Sarmatian tribesmen, who were both the allies and the enemies of the Romans are believed to be the ancestors of the Poles.

POSTSCRIPT

I

The Sound was barely audible,
like the gentle noise
made by the metal horse-trappings
as the muscles of the animals
lurched slowly forward
with the movement of their hooves.
In late autumn,
the tall feather - grass of the Steppes
was dried out,
giving way to the hooves unwillingly...
The Nomad Saka Cavalry
came upon a huge burial kurgan,
a mound of earth worn away by time.

II

The top layer of the earthen mound
had been blown away
by the wind of the Steppes,
exposing the death-guard
of a fallen Saka king.
The riders who were still erect
sat upon the saddled bones
of their horses -
tattered remnants of clothing
that still clung to the bodies
of the death-guard fluttered in the wind.
Small silver bells hung from their horses,
from the worn leather death-masks
of their mounts -
as the bells moved with the wind,
they played a hollow, haunting tune.

III

At those Royal gates of Nineveh,
I stood as though transfixed;
spellbound looking up, ever higher
to the great stone statues
of the sacred Winged Bulls, the Lamassi
The winged Lamassu had long muscular legs,
the hooves of bulls, the paws of lions
like powerful animals in their stride.
The great stone wings made the gods look
as though they were in flight,
like some kind of giant eagles.
High above the wings, the rock hard gods
wore the tall Royal Assyrian crowns.
The winged gods
had the faces of the kings of Ashur...
the long, stony beards combined
the strength of the bulls and the lions
with the deity
of the Royal House of Assyria.

IV

Dawn on the northern shore,
on the ancient shore of the Black Sea.
Tent-Nomads take their herds to pasture,
as a flowing sea of Nomad Horse-Bowmen
rides the flowing Steppe-lands.
In the royal tent of the Nomad Chieftain,
enemy skulls filled with molten gold
rest on the colorful carpet,
on the red and gold woven carpet
decorated with royal Golden Stags.
The Chieftain's horse, a small Mongol pony
has enemy scalps, hanging from its bridle.

The Nomad god of the sun, Oetosyrus
gleams in the dawn from the royal shield,
gleams in the dawn from the sacred Golden Stag.
Dusk on the northern shore,
on the ancient shore of the Black Sea.
The Nomads, a flowing sea of ox-drawn
house-wagons,
of black felt tents, vanish
in the frozen sea of time.

www.ingramcontent.com/pod-product-compliance
Lightning Source LLC
Chambersburg PA
CBHW052130110526
44592CB00013B/1828